Seven Steps to Receiving

the Holy Spirit

BY KENNETH E. HAGIN

Tenth Printing - 1978

Kenneth E. Hagin Evangelistic Association, Inc.
P. O. Box 50126
Tulsa, Oklahoma 74150   U.S.A.

ISBN 0-89276-003-6

CONTENTS

CHAPTER 1

SEVEN STEPS TO RECEIVING THE HOLY SPIRIT

John 14:16, 17: "And I will pray the Father, and he shall give you another Comforter, that he may abide with you for ever; Even the Spirit of truth, whom the world cannot receive, because it seeth him not, neither knoweth him; but ye know him; for he dwelleth with you, and shall be in you."

Acts 2:32, 33: "This Jesus hath God raised up, whereof we all are witnesses. Therefore being by the right hand of God exalted, and having received of the Father the promise of the Holy Ghost, he hath shed forth this, which ye now see and hear."

WHAT CAN WE DO TO HELP A PERSON RECEIVE THE HOLY SPIRIT?

(1) We must help the candidate to see that God has *already given* the Holy Spirit and that it is up to *him* (the candidate) to receive the Holy Spirit now! Tell the candidate that he is not to beg God. We are His children and begging our heavenly Father is unnecessary and is actually evidence of unbelief.

(2) Lead the candidate to see that now that he is saved, he is ready to receive the Holy Spirit. So many people have been taught wrongly and they think there is much that they have to do before they are ready to receive. Some think they have to get "straight" before they can receive. But if a person is saved, he *is* "straight" and is ready to receive the Holy Spirit. The *sinner* cannot change his nature, but when he is "Born Again" he *is* changed and has become a new creature in Christ Jesus.

Illustration: Moody tells the story of a young woman who liked to dance. She felt she could never give it up and therefore could not be saved. But she was encouraged to come to church and get saved, and then told that after that she could dance just as much as she wanted to. She found to her amazement that after she was saved, the desire to dance had left her. The "want to" was gone!

3

Yes, we can lie or steal or do any other type of sin that we want to after we are saved but we just *don't want* to any more. "If any man be in Christ, he is a new creature. Old things are passed away." Things that we once liked, do not appeal to us any longer because our *nature* is changed. Therefore, if a person is "born again" he will never be anymore saved than he is right then. So, he is ready *right then* to receive the Holy Spirit.

(3) Even if a believer doesn't have the ministry of "laying on of hands," it is still allright for him to help the candidate in this way as it releases the candidate's faith. Some are gifted, or given the gift of "laying on of hands" for people to receive the Holy Spirit and healing. This gift is given by God and cannot be bought with money. Acts 8:18-20: "And when Simon saw that through laying on of the apostles' hands the Holy Ghost was given. he offered them money, Saying, Give me also this power, that on whomsoever I lay hands. he may receive the Holy Ghost. But Peter said unto him, Thy money perish with thee, because thou hast thought that the gift of God may be purchased with money." However, when a Spirit-filled believer lays hands upon a candidate, he cannot *give* the candidate the Holy Spirit. The candidate has to *receive for himself;* we cannot do it for him. In the same way, no one can receive healing for us but our own will is what comes into place. We have to take these things ourselves. We can minister through the Word on salvation and on the other promises of God, but the hearer must receive it himself. When we preach the Word of God, people become convicted but that is as far as we can go. Our praying can bring God's *power* on people, but they must *receive* on their own. "That is mine! I receive it! I take it!"

(4) Tell the candidate that *he* is to speak! The Holy Spirit will act upon his vocal organs (lips and tongue) but the candidate must put the sound to the action and speak out. Acts 19:6: "And when Paul had laid his hands upon them, the Holy Ghost came on them; and *they* spake with tongues, and prophesied." It is to be expected that when the candidate receives the Holy Spirit that he will speak in tongues as the Spirit gives utterance. The Holy Ghost does not talk in tongues. *We* do the talking. The Holy Ghost does not *take our tongues* and talk; *we* do the talking. Acts 2:4: "And they were all filled with the Holy Ghost, and began to speak with other tongues, as the Spirit gave them utterance." *"They"* is the subject of the sentence. *They* did the talking. The Holy Spirit gave them the utterance. Acts 10:44-46: "While Peter yet spake these words, the Holy Ghost fell on all them which heard the word. And they of the cir-

4

cumcision which believed were astonished, as many as came with Peter, because that on the Gentiles also was poured out the gift of the Holy Ghost. For they heard them speak with tongues, and magnify God . . . " Acts 19:6: "And when Paul laid his hands upon them, the Holy Ghost came on them; and *they* spake with tongues, and prophesied."

In I Cor. 14:2-15, 18, 27, Paul *always* refers to the individual in his instructions to the Church. "I thank my God. *I* speak with tongues more than *ye* all . . . He that speaketh in an unknown tongue . . . If any *man* speak in an unknown tongue . . . ," etc. The word 'unknown' as used here is in italics and has been *added* to the original text from the Greek by the translators thinking to help the readers realize that to *us* the tongue (or language) was unknown but, of course, it is not unknown to God. Also, as Paul points out in this text, it is certainly profitable to talk to ourselves and to God in tongues. This is Scriptural and blessed. Nowhere in the New Testament does it state that the Holy Spirit is speaking in tongues. Always the *individual* does the speaking but the Holy Spirit gives the utterance. Speaking in tongues (privately) edifies the believer or builds him up. But Paul said in Verse 19 of I Cor. 14: "Yet *in the church* I had rather speak five words with my understanding, that by my voice I might teach others also, than ten thousand words in an unknown tongue." Here he was referring to preaching and teaching. His listeners would profit nothing if he spoke in tongues in the public assembly because they could not understand him. Therefore, he says, it would be better to speak five words with understanding in order to teach.

Be sure that in dealing with a candidate, only Bible language is used — *not* man's manufactured expressions; otherwise, the instructions become confusing, and sometimes even frightening, to the candidate.

(5) Tell the candidate to throw away all of his fears that he has acquired from foolish teachers that have made him afraid. Tell him not to fear receiving something which is false or counterfeit. There is no danger of receiving anything false. God does not lie and He said that if we ask, He will give the Holy Spirit to us. Luke 11:11-13: "If a son shall ask bread of any of you that is a father, will he give him a stone? or if he ask a fish, will he for a fish give him a serpent? Or if he shall ask an egg, will he offer him a scorpion? If ye then, being evil, know how to give good gifts unto your children: how much more shall your heavenly Father give the Holy Spirit to

5

them that ask him?" Help the individual to realize that he will receive the *real* Holy Spirit.

(6) Tell him to open his mouth wide and to breathe in as deeply as possible and to tell God in his spirit, "I am receiving the Holy Ghost right now by faith." Insist that he must not speak a single word in English. You can't talk two languages at once. The mind cannot enter into this experience; it comes from the heart. When you see the Spirit move upon the lips, tell him to speak *boldly* whatever seems easiest for him. When that person has lifted his voice in faith and believed God and when he can hear himself speaking in a clear language, then he knows that he has received the Holy Spirit. Job 29:21-23: "Unto me men gave ear, and waited, and kept silence at my counsel. After my words they spake not again; and my speech dropped upon them. And they waited for me as for the rain; and they opened their mouth wide as for the latter rain." James 5:7: "Be patient therefore, brethren, unto the coming of the Lord. Behold, the husbandman waiteth for the precious fruit of the earth, and hath long patience for it, until he receive the early and latter rain." Hosea 6:3: "Then shall we know, if we follow on to know the Lord: his going forth is prepared as the morning; and he shall come unto us as the rain, as the latter and former rain unto the earth." The "latter rain" and the "former rain" are the Holy Ghost. The "early rain" fell at Pentecost. We have been enjoying the "latter rain".

Jesus said, "Come and drink," and He was speaking about the Holy Spirit. When a person takes a drink of water, he opens his mouth and takes a breath. You can't take a drink of water with your mouth closed and you can't receive the Holy Ghost with your mouth closed. Speaking in tongues is actually co-operation between you and the Holy Spirit.

HOW DOES THE HOLY SPIRIT GUIDE US?

There are two ways:

Many people experience the hearing of the supernatural words forming way down inside their inner being and the words bubble up until they are spoken through the mouth.

The other way is by a fluttering of the lips. The candidate feels a tightening of the jaw and the person's tongue feels thick. The Holy Spirit does this because the lips and tongue are the organs we use to form words. But, we have to put the sound to it ourselves. That is the way He gives us utterance or the way he prompts us.

6

You get *full* by drinking. Eph. 5:18, 19: "And be not drunk with wine, wherein is excess; but be *filled* with the Spirit; Speaking to yourselves in psalms and hymns and spiritual songs, singing and making melody in your heart to the Lord." The "spiritual songs" spoken of here do *not* mean songs out of our song books, but instantaneous songs which are given on the spur of the moment by the Holy Spirit.

The word "inspiration" means breathing in the Spirit of God. You can look up to God and breathe Him in. By having the candidate breathe deeply, he can thus relax and "drink in" the Holy Ghost or be *filled* with the Holy Ghost.

(7) Never crowd around the person who has come to receive the Holy Ghost and never permit a crowd to gather around him. There have been many instances in Full Gospeldom where people have gathered around a candidate and acted in this manner: One person on the right would shout in the candidate's ear, "Hang on!" The person on the left would shout, "Turn loose!" Another person would pound him on the back and shout, "Die out!" In *spite* of this (bless their ignorant hearts) the candidate would receive the Holy Spirit — not *because* of it, but in spite of it! This is ignorance, pure and simple and in many cases has cheated the candidate out of the blessing because it has frightened him half to death and he goes away and *never does* receive the Holy Ghost.

If you feel that it is necessary to pray out loud, do *not* pray in English; pray only in tongues as this will strengthen the faith of the candidate.

7

CHAPTER II

TEN REASONS WHY EVERY BELIEVER SHOULD SPEAK IN TONGUES

In I Corinthians 14:18, Paul says, "I thank my God, I speak with tongues more than ye all."

I want to go on record with Paul in saying, "I thank my God, I speak with tongues."

You know, if Paul spoke in tongues more than the Corinthians did, he must have done a great amount of it. He must have awakened speaking in tongues, gone to bed speaking in tongues, and spoken in tongues between meals. It seems as if that is about all some Corinthians wanted to do was to speak in tongues. He certainly did a tremendous amount of speaking in tongues.

I want to give you ten reasons why every believer should speak in tongues:

1. We know that the Word of God teaches us that when we are filled with the Holy Ghost, we do speak with other tongues as the Spirit of God gives utterance. It is the initial evidence or sign of the Holy Spirit indwelling. Acts 2:4 says, "And they were all filled with the Holy Ghost, and began to speak with other tongues, as the Spirit gave them utterance."

Then you will find Paul, in writing to the Corinthian church, counseled them to continue their practice of speaking in tongues in their worship of God and in their prayer life. He stated in I Cor. 14:4, that "he that speaketh in an unknown tongue edifieth himself." So speaking or praying in tongues is a means of spiritual edification or building up.

Howard Carter, who was General Superintendent of the Assemblies of God of Great Britain for nineteen years, was the founder of the oldest Pentecostal Bible school in the world. He said that we must not forget that the speaking with other tongues is not only the initial evidence of the Holy Spirit's indwelling but is a continual experience for the rest of one's life. For what purpose? To assist in the worship of God. Speaking in tongues is a flowing stream that should never dry up, for it will enrich a person's life spiritually.

He was correct in his statement. Paul says speaking in tongues will edify you or build you up spiritually.

2. I Corinthians 14:2 says, "For he that speaketh in an unknown tongue speaketh not unto men, but unto God: for no man understandeth him; howbeit in the spirit he speaketh mysteries." Weymouth's translation of the New Testament says that, "he speaks divine secrets."

Paul is saying here that God has given to the church a divine supernatural means of communication with God. Praise the Lord! Paul stated in the 14th verse of this same chapter, "For if I pray in an unknown tongue, my spirit prayeth, but my understanding is unfruitful." Notice that he said, "My spirit prayeth." The Amplified Testament adds, my Spirit by the Holy Spirit within me prays." Jesus said, "God is a Spirit." You see, when you pray in tongues, your spirit prays. When you pray in tongues, your spirit is in direct contact with God who is a spirit, and you are talking to Him in a divine supernatural language. Praise God!

It is amazing how intelligent people can ask in the light of these Scriptures, "What is the value of speaking in tongues?" It almost makes one doubt their intelligence. Many people have asked me this question, knowing all the time what the Scriptures teach.

Friend, there is a value in speaking in tongues — a great value. If a person cannot see this, then there has to be something wrong with his understanding. I don't mean that he should see it because he has spoken with tongues. I saw it as a Baptist minister before I ever spoke with tongues. I began to see what the Word said.

I remember I visited a Full Gospel service when I was not busy with my own church, because they preached divine healing. You see I had been raised up from a deathbed and healed by the power of God, and there was just something about fellowshipping with people that believed like I did that stimulated my faith. A person must have that fellowship. Therefore, I would visit with them. Of course, they taught speaking in tongues as the Holy Spirit gave utterance. At first I did not see the light on the Holy Ghost, but as I began to study the Scriptures, I began to see.

I visited the home of some denominational people who had an only child, a daughter, who was a pianist. The Full Gospel people there were having a tent revival. They did not have a pianist, and this young lady had volunteered her services. After they built a church,

9

since they still did not have a pianist, she continued to play for them. When they began to preach tongues, the young lady's mother became quite concerned. She told me because of this she thought she would not let her daughter play in the church any longer.

I suggested that she read what the Bible had to say about it. Instead, she wanted to read what her church discipline had to say about it. I told her that it did not mention it, as I had already read it. Then she said she would ask her pastor. I told her that there was no need of that because he did not believe in it and was not even saved. She looked at me with amazement, and I told her that a man who would curse his mother, as I knew he had done, and treat her as this man did was not saved and that I did not care what church he pastored. If he carried on in this manner, he was not saved. Even a gentleman would not have done what he did, much less a Christian.

Needless to say, this dear woman did not take my advice. She took her daughter out of the Full Gospel Church, and the girl began attending where this unsaved man pastored. They had church-sponsored drinking and dancing. Any church, and I say this boldly, regardless of denomination, that advocates this type of thing is wrong according to the Word of God. While at a church dance, this girl got drunk, ended up pregnant, and had an illegitimate child. They were of a family that had a good social standing in this small town. Because of their daughter, the father died at the age of about forty-one and the mother ended up in the state hospital for the insane.

You see, she said she had some friends with whom she intended to discuss speaking in tongues. She did, and of course they did not point her to the Bible. You can readily see how important it is for us to walk in the light of what the Bible has to say about a subject, not by what our friends would suggest. Friends, how much better it would have been for that daughter to have stayed on that piano bench in a church where they did not have drinking or dancing.

If God says speaking in tongues is of value, then it is of value. If God says that it edifies, then it does edify us. If God says that it is a supernatural means of communication with Himself, then it is a supernatural means of communication with Himself. Amen! If God says every believer should speak in tongues, then every believer should speak in tongues. Jesus did not say that just a few should speak in tongues. He said, "And these signs shall follow them that believe." "Them" is plural. That means all. One of these signs was, "They shall speak with new tongues."

10

3. Speaking in tongues is a supernatural evidence of the Holy Spirit's indwelling. In Acts 10 in Cornelius' household, the six brethren of the circumcision who had come with Peter were astonished because on the Gentiles also was poured out the gift of the Holy Ghost. They thought it was only for the Jewish church. How did they know the Gentiles had received the gift of the Holy Ghost? Acts 10:46 says, "For they heard them speak with tongues and magnify God." In other words, that was the supernatural or initial evidence that the Holy Ghost is indwelling, but continued practice of speaking in tongues and praying in tongues helps us to be conscious of His presence. If I can be conscious of the indwelling presence of the Holy Ghost within me every day, then it is certain to affect the way that I live. Praise God!

A Full Gospel minister told me about holding a meeting for a pastor. This pastor and his wife lived in an apartment near the church. They had a young girl about twelve years old. One day as was his usual routine, he had gone to mail some letters and had come back from his daily walk. He heard this girl fussing at her mother, and she was really having a tantrum about something she wanted to do. When the girl saw him, she fell to her knees and began to cry and to apologize to him for his having seen her conduct herself that way. He told her that was all right and led her to the church altar to pray with her. He explained that he was only an evangelist, but for her to remember that there was One greater than he who always heard her and knew how she acted, and that was the Holy Ghost that was dwelling in her life. He always saw and heard her. She repented of her conduct and was saved and filled with the Holy Ghost.

A few years later, she had grown up considerably, and upon his return to their church, she told him that she had never forgotten his words and that she had never lost her temper again in such a manner. He had told her to pray daily in tongues because it helps one to be conscious of God's presence in his life. This had helped her to overcome her temper.

Someone says, "Well, I know a person that has been saved and filled with the Holy Ghost, and they lose their temper and say things they should not." Yes, I do too. But I can say one thing: they have not prayed in tongues that day and been in fellowship with God. I know something from my own experience. It is awfully easy, when one is not conscious of His presence, to become aggravated and exasperated. But if that person will take time to fellowship with Him,

11

speaking in tongues and praying, then he can be conscious of His indwelling and will not do or say things he otherwise would.

4. Praying in tongues eliminates selfishness entering into our prayers. If I pray out of my own thinking, it may be unscriptural, and it may be selfish. I think too many times our prayers are like the old farmer's prayers. He would pray, "God bless me and my wife, my son John, his wife, us four, and no more."

We don't say it in just those words, but that is actually what it amounts to when it is all said and done. Paul said in Romans 8:26, "For we know not what we should pray for as we ought."

"We know not" for what to pray as we ought. He did not say we did not know how to pray, because we do know how to pray. We pray to the Father in the name of the Lord Jesus Christ. This is *how* to pray. But just because I know *how* to pray doesn't mean I know *for what to pray* as I should. Paul says, "For we know not what we should pray for as we ought: but the Spirit himself maketh intercession for us with groanings which cannot be uttered."

P. C. Nelson, the founder of Southwestern Bible Institute, was a Greek scholar. He told his young ministers that the Greek literally reads, "The Holy Spirit maketh intercession for us with groanings which cannot be uttered in articulate speech." Articulate speech means your ordinary kind of speech. He pointed out that the Greek bears out that this not only included groanings in prayer but also in other tongues. Well, that agrees with what Paul said in I Corinthians 14:14, "For if I pray in an unknown tongue, my spirit prayeth, but my understanding is unfruitful." The Amplified Testament says, "My spirit by the Holy Spirit within me prays."

People had better be careful about making fun of speaking in tongues, because when you pray in tongues, it is your spirit praying by the Holy Spirit that is within you. They are actually making fun of the Holy Ghost. It is the Holy Spirit within you giving you the utterance, and you are speaking it out of your spirit. You do the talking, and He gives the utterance. By that method the Holy Spirit then is helping you to pray according to the will of God for the things which should be prayed for. "We know not what we should pray for as we ought."

Now this is not something that the Holy Ghost does apart from you. He does not groan or speak in tongues apart from you. Those groanings come up from inside of you and escape your lips. The Holy Ghost is not going to do your praying. He is sent to dwell in you. He is a helper, and He is an intercessor, but He does not inter-

12

cede apart from you. He is not responsible for your prayer life, but He was sent to help you to pray. He is sent to help you to get the job done. Praise God!

He will help us. The way He helps us in our praying is by those groanings that come out of our spirit born of the Holy Spirit that escape our lips. And speaking in tongues is praying as the Spirit gives utterance. It is Spirit-directed praying. It eliminates the possibility of selfish praying that enters into our prayers.

Many times when people are praying out of their own minds, they will be given things that are actually not the will of God and are not best for them. You don't believe that? Then you don't believe the Bible. If God's people want things a certain way, even though it is not best for them and it is not God's will, He will permit it. I can prove that to you. God did not want Israel to have a king. He told them so, but they wanted a king, and He permitted them to have one. That was not His highest will; it was not best for them. Isn't that right?

Sometime ago I had been praying in the Spirit for about two and a half hours, which seemed like fifteen minutes. While in the Spirit I had placed one fist on top of the other; then there seemed to be a pull that would tip my hands to one side. With all my strength I tried to straigthen up my fists, but invariably they would be pulled over to one side again. The same thing happened three times. Then the Spirit of God said to me, "People by their wrong praying pull things out of focus." "For we know not what to pray for as we ought." So by their own praying, by their own thinking, and out of their own mind, they pull things out of focus. This then, gets God's plan out of line or focus many times, and then His perfect will cannot be wrought. One thing you can be sure of: When you are praying in tongues you can keep everything in line, everything in focus. You are praying according to the will of God and to the interests of all involved. I tell you that was a revelation. I knew it in a sense before, but I had never seen the necessity of praying in tongues as I did then.

5. Speaking in tongues helps me to learn to trust God more fully. It will help my faith to speak in tongues. No, it will not give me faith. I said it would help my faith. Jude 1:20 says, "But ye, beloved, building up yourselves on your most holy faith, praying in the Holy Ghost." There is conclusive proof. It will help and it will stimulate my faith. It helps me to learn more fully how to trust God. Why? Since the Holy Spirit supernaturally directs the words I speak, faith

13

must be exercised in order to speak with tongues because I do not know what the next word will be. I am trusting God for that. And trusting God in one line will help me to trust God in another line.

As a Baptist minister, I pastored a community church. Everyone came—Methodists, Baptists, Presbyterians, and all denominations. Actually it was the only church in the community, so everyone came. I stayed in the home of a fine dear Methodist Christian. This woman had an ulcerated stomach. The doctors felt that it would surely turn into cancer. I knew God could and would heal her, but somehow I was never able to lift her faith up to that point. She ate only a little food and milk and could never seem to keep that on her stomach. But one day a wonderful thing happened! She received the infilling of the Holy Ghost. I came in, and she was eating foods and drinks she had never been able to eat before. God had not only healed her, but He had filled her with the Holy Ghost.

I have seen many people who have had this type of experience. What is the connection? We know that just receiving the Baptism of the Holy Ghost does not heal you, but speaking with tongues will help you to learn more fully how to trust God. So when you speak in tongues, it helps you to believe God for other things because it stimulates your faith.

6. Speaking in tongues is a means of keeping you free from contamination with the ungodly, the profane and all the vulgar talk around you, if you are working on a job or out in the public. You can speak with tongues to yourself. When you come to church, or for that matter, regardless of where you may be, you can do as I Corinthians 14:28 says, "Speak to himself, and to God." The whole verse reads, "But if there be no interpreter, let him keep silence in the church: and let him speak to himself, and to God." What is He talking about? The 27th verse says, "If any man speak in an unknown tongue, let it be by two, or at the most by three, and that by course: and let one interpret." But if there is no interpreter present, then you just keep silent in the church and speak to yourself and to God. If you can do that in the church, then you can do it on the job. You would not disturb anyone. I have done that many times. I do not work out, but I have been in the barber shop or downtown where I have heard things that do not help in one's spiritual life. No matter where you are, you can speak to yourself and to God. This will keep you from being contaminated with the things of the world.

7. Speaking in tongues provides a way for things to be prayed for,

14

but for which no one thinks to pray about or about which they know nothing. The Holy Spirit knows everything. The Word says, "But the Spirit Himself helpeth our infirmities, making intercession for us with groanings which cannot be uttered in articulate speech." In that is included speaking with tongues.

There were two young Assemblies of God men from England who were missionaries to Africa. One was home in England after a missionary tour. A young woman asked him if he kept a diary. He said, "Yes."

About two years prior, this young woman had been awakened during the night, and she felt an urgency to pray. She prayed for about one hour in tongues. Then she had a vision of a grass hut. He was the only white person—the rest were natives. She saw him die, and the natives covered him up, then went outside. Suddenly, she saw him come out of the hut and stand in their midst. All of the natives began to rejoice.

She asked him if he had had an experience like that. After they had compared notes, dates, and made allowances for the difference of time, they found out that all this took place at the exact time. Praise God! They had no connection with one another. She only knew that he was a missionary and that is all. You see, he had contracted one of those deadly fevers, and his partner was in another territory at that time, leaving him alone. But the Spirit of God provides a way for things to be prayed for that should be prayed for, because the Holy Ghost knows everything. Amen!

Another missionary to Africa that I have heard on a number of occasions told of an experience he had. He and a native worker had hired a man with his boat to go to another island to preach the gospel. On the way back, suddenly a tropical storm or squall came up. The wind was really blowing and tossing the boat about. The owner told them that if they stayed out there, they would turn over and drown, and yet if they went ashore, they would hit the reefs. He asked the missionary what he wanted to do. The missionary replied, "It is your boat. What do you want to do, and what do you think would be best?"

The man answered that he would take a chance with the reefs. The missionary and his native worker had prayer and said, "All right, let's go." He reported as they neared the reefs, suddenly it felt as though the boat was lifted up and carried over the water. You see, it was night, and the boat was a sailboat. The missionary said he, the native worker, and the two or three sinners, one of them

15

being the owner, were witnesses to this miraculous event. God literally lifted this boat up over the reefs and into the waters that were safe.

The following week he was at a certain missionary station and another missionary, a woman, asked him if he had been in trouble the past Monday night about ten o'clock. He asked her why. She said that she had gone to bed rather early that night as she had been planning on leaving the following morning on a trip. About ten o'clock she was awakened and had such a burden to pray that all she could do was pray in tongues and groan in the Spirit. She said, "I did not know what it was, but I seemed to have the impression that you were in trouble, and I just had to pray for you." He then told her what had happened, and it was at the exact time she was praying. Praise God! The Spirit knows.

In May, 1956, I was in California. We had a three bedroom trailer house then, as our children, a boy and a girl, were with us, and they were teen-agers. During the night I was awakened. It seemed as though someone had laid hands on me. I wondered if someone was in the room. I looked at my wife, and she was sleeping soundly. Everything else was fine. Yet my heart was beating wildly as though I were scared. So I said, "Lord, what is the matter? There is something wrong somewhere. What is it? Oh Holy Spirit, you are everywhere, and you know everything, so give me the utterance."

I began to pray with tongues. I prayed to myself and to God, and my wife just kept on sleeping. I prayed for about an hour. Then I began to laugh and sing a little in tongues — in the Spirit. You see when you pray in this manner, always keep at it until you have a note of praise, and then whatever it is you are praying about, as we say in the natural, you have prayed through. You will either laugh, be joyous, or sing. I knew whatever it was I was praying about had come to pass. I had the answer. I then went to sleep.

While I was asleep, I had a dream. In this dream I saw my youngest brother in a hotel room in Louisiana. No one told me that he was in Louisiana, but I knew he was there. I saw him awaken a little after midnight. I saw them summon a doctor, and he was carried away in an ambulance. I saw the red light flashing as they took him to the hospital. In the dream, I stood in the corridor outside his door. His door was shut. The doctor came out of his room. He then shook my hand and said, "He is dead. He is dead."

I replied, "No doctor, he is not dead."

He asked, "What do you mean, he is not dead?"

16

I said, "The Lord told me he would live and not die."

The doctor became angry then and said, "Well, smart aleck, come with me and I will show you that he is dead. I have pronounced too many people dead not to know when someone is dead." He then took me by the arm and led me into my brother's room. He walked over to the bed and jerked the sheet back. When he did, my brother's eyes opened, and he saw my brother breathing. He began to stutter and said, "Why, you knew something I did not know." He was astonished and just kept saying over and over, "He is alive, isn't he?" In my dream, I saw my brother rise from bed, and he was well. That, you see, was what I was praying about.

I had no word from anyone regarding my family. In August, we went back to Texas. Just as I finished parking my trailer, my brother came up, as he saw I had just arrived. We began to talk. He said, "I almost died while you were gone."

I answered, "Yes, I know." He asked if mother had told me. I told him I had not talked to anyone, as I had just come in and that no one had written me anything.

He then asked, "How did you know that I nearly died?" I told him how he had taken sick in the night time and all about it. He assured me that it happened just as I said. He said that he was unconscious for about forty minutes, but the doctors had thought he was dead. They had pronounced him dead.

Friends, I had no means of communication in my trailer. I did not have a phone. But praise God this is God's original communication system! Yes, it is scriptural, and it is biblical. We should all pray in this manner, because then we pray for things about which we know nothing.

8. Isaiah 28:11-12 says, "For with stammering lips and another tongue will he speak to this people. To whom he said, This is the rest wherewith ye may cause the weary to rest; and this is the refreshing; yet they would not hear." What is the rest? Speaking with other tongues. This is the rest wherewith ye may cause the weary to rest; and this is the refreshing. What is the rest? What is the refreshing? This speaking with other tongues, God's Word said. Sometimes the doctor says you need a rest cure. Well, I'll tell you the best one in the world. Many times you take a vacation and have to rest up after you come home in order to get back on the job. But isn't this wonderful? You can just take this rest cure every day. Praise God! In these days of turmoil, insecurity, and perplexity, we

17

need this rest and refreshing, and it comes by speaking with other tongues. Glory!

9. I Corinthians 14:15-17 says, "What is it then? I will pray with the spirit, and I will pray with the understanding also: I will sing with the spirit, and I will sing with the understanding also. Else when thou shalt bless with the spirit, how shall he that occupieth the room of the unlearned say 'Amen' at thy giving of thanks, seeing he understandeth not what thou sayest? For thou verily givest thanks well, but the other is not edified."

For instance, you invite me to eat with you tomorrow and say, "Brother Hagin, give thanks please." Paul said he that occupieth the room of the unlearned (he is speaking about people that are unlearned in spiritual things) would not be edified if I prayed in tongues, for they would not understand. So he said it would be better to pray with my understanding there, but if I did pray in tongues I am supposed to interpret it, so that they would know what I said.

Notice that he said, "Thou verily givest thanks well, but the other is not edified." In other words, that is really the best way to pray and give thanks, Paul says. But in the presence of people that are unlearned, offer your thanks with your understanding also that they may be edified. Then they will be edified because they hear and know what you said. I want you to notice though that Paul said speaking with tongues provides the most perfect way to pray and to give thanks because he said, "for thou verily givest thanks well."

10. James 3:8 says, "But the tongue can no man tame; it is an unruly evil, full of deadly poison." Speaking with other tongues, yielding your tongue to the Holy Spirit to speak with other tongues is a long step toward fully yielding all of your members to God. For if you can yield your tongue, you can yield any member. That's what the Scripture teaches.

I want us to realize that there is also what we call a "public side" to tongues. First, people speak with other tongues when they receive the Holy Ghost in public. Those around Peter and the 120 heard them speak with tongues. Second, the church is edified when someone speaks with other tongues in public assembly with interpretation.

Paul plainly stated that to prophesy is to speak unto men to edification, exhortation, and comfort. But he said greater is he that prophesies than he that speaks with tongues except he interprets. In that case, he is saying that tongues with interpretation is equal to prophecy. Using a natural term as an example, it takes two nickels to

18

make a dime, but you know that two nickels are not a ten cent piece. What Paul is saying is that prophecy is the dime or the ten cent piece. Naturally, it would be better to have the dime than to have the nickels. If prophesying is speaking unto men to edification, exhortation, and comfort, right here let me say that prophesying is *not preaching,* regardless of what anyone tells you. There can sometimes be an element of prophecy in preaching, but these are supernatural gifts. If prophesying were preaching, you would not have to make any preparation to preach. But you have to study to preach. Paul said to study to show yourself approved unto God. Amen! You do not have to study to speak with tongues and to interpret, nor do you have to study to prophesy. It comes by inspiration of the Spirit. Of course, when one is preaching under the inspiration of the Holy Spirit, and then suddenly says things he never thought of, then it is true, this is inspiration, and this is an element of prophecy. Prophesying is just simply inspirational supernatural utterance in a known tongue. It is, in other words, what tongues with interpretation is. Interpretation is inspirational supernatural speech in a known tongue that tells what has been said in speaking with other tongues. Tongues is a supernatural utterance in an unknown tongue.

Third, when used in line with the Word, speaking with tongues with interpretation convinces the unbeliever of the reality of the presence of God and often causes him to turn to God to be saved. I have seen this take place many times. Fourth, Jesus said, "These signs shall follow them that believe. In my name shall they cast out devils (that can be in private or public), they shall lay hands on the sick and they shall recover and they shall speak with new tongues." Praise God!

Of course, you do not want only prolonged praying in tongues in the service, because without interpretation, the audience does not know what is being said and thus is not being edified. But when you come to the altar, it is all right to pray with tongues all you want. You came to the altar to get edified, you see. If we are all lifting our hands and praying in the regular service, then it is all right to pray in tongues. But when the congregation ceases to pray, then you should cease too. We should know just how to use what we have to the greatest advantage.

Now you may ask, "How can I speak with tongues?" Many say you do not have to tell anyone how to speak with tongues because the Holy Ghost speaks. No, the Holy Ghost does not. The Holy Ghost merely gives the utterance, and you do the speaking. We are

19

confused in the Full Gospel circles. We more or less have a "language" all our own, and it is confusing to the person just entering into our circle. We have to be careful how we tell a person to receive the Holy Ghost.

One day I stopped in a drug store to have a bite to eat. I ordered a pimento cheese sandwich and a vanilla malt. The girl called out to the cook, "A Palm Beach and a Van Duz."

I thought to myself, "I did not order that, but I will wait to see what I get. If that is not what I ordered, I will not accept it." However, soon she came out with a pimento cheese sandwich and a vanilla malt. You see, they had a language all their own, though I did not know what she was saying. Sometimes we are like that. We have a language of our own in the church world. Maybe we know what we mean, and maybe we don't. But we do confuse others. Rather than having a language of our own, I think it is better just to come back to the Bible and say it as the Bible says. Amen!

Now I know many times you have heard someone say, "Just let the Holy Ghost speak." But the Holy Ghost does not do the talking. You do it. The Holy Ghost gives you the utterance, and you are the one that speaks it.

One night I was holding a meeting in a large church, and after services my wife and I, the pastor and his wife went out for sandwiches. The pastor's wife said, "Brother Hagin, I do not agree with you." I told her I was always open to anyone's helping me with the Scripture and the Word of God. (Anyone teaching should be open and have a teachable spirit, or they should not be teaching. I mean open toward the Word of God, not a person's opinion. We are to preach the Word, not opinions nor convictions. I have no time for those that think that they know everything and do not know anything. I do not know everything but I praise God for what I do know. Amen! The Bible says, "We know in part and we prophesy in part." Thank God for the part I do know.)

I asked, "What is it on which you do not agree with me?"

She answered, "I disagree with you about your saying that the Holy Ghost does not speak in tongues."

"That is right, and I will have to disagree with you, because that is what the Word of God teaches."

She said, "I believe it just like the Bible said it."

I asked her how the Bible said it. She replied, "The Bible says, for when He is come, He shall speak for himself."

I said, "I would believe that too if it were in the Bible."

"Why Brother Hagin, I am an ordained minister, and I know what the Bible says."

"I am an ordained minister too, but everything that I have said down through the years has not all been so."

She continued, "I have preached that for 25 years."

I told her, "You have preached something that was not so for 25 years."

She added, "I have heard that preached and heard it quoted in the prayer room for 25 years."

"That still does not make it so, for there are many things preached and quoted that are not so." I asked her to show this to me in the Bible. She said she would have to find it in her Bible, and she did not have it with her. I asked her how long it would take to find it, and she said that it would not take more than ten minutes.

I told her to call me when she found it, as we were staying at a certain hotel there in town. She agreed. You know friends, nine years have come and gone, and she has not called me yet. Why? Because there is no Scripture in the Bible that says, "When the Holy Spirit is come, He shall speak for himself." I had told her that I would give her three hundred dollars if she found that in the Bible. The closest thing to a Scripture like that is where it says, "When he is come he shall speak not of himself, but whatsoever he shall hear that shall he speak; he shall take the things of mine and show them to you." Jesus said this.

No, the Holy Ghost does not speak. Man does the speaking, but the Holy Ghost supernaturally directs it. Acts 2:4 says, "And they were all filled with the Holy Ghost and began to speak with other tongues." *They* began to speak with other tongues as the Spirit gave *them* utterance. He gave them utterance and they did the talking. Weymouth's translation reads, "They began to speak as the Spirit gave them words to utter." Another translation reads, "They began to speak with other tongues as the Spirit prompted them to speak." Moffat's translation reads, "They began to speak with other tongues as the Spirit enabled them to express themselves." *They* (the believers) were doing it; the Spirit gave it to *them*.

Speaking with tongues is based on the act of the human will. The fact that you speak is not supernatural, but the supernatural part is what is being said and from where it is coming. Notice that Paul says in I Cor. 14:14,15, " . . . if I pray in an unknown tongue, my

21

spirit prayeth, but my understanding is unfruitful. What is it then? *I* will pray with the spirit (that is with tongues) and *I* will pray with the understanding."

If I ask, "Can you stay and pray at the altar?" and you reply, "I will stay, and I will pray," you can pray with your understanding because you say, "I will."

The Spirit-filled believer can also say, "I will pray with the spirit." Your will enters into your decision to pray with the spirit just as much as it does when you pray with your understanding. That is Biblical.

Paul also says, 'I thank my God *I* speak with tongues." He did not say the Holy Ghost speaks through me. You do not find such expressions in the New Testament anywhere. Paul said, *I* speak with tongues."

Many times people say, "Well, that was just I talking in tongues." How true! Yes, it is you because it is not I, if you are the one doing the talking. Yes, you are the one speaking with tongues as the Holy Spirit gives you the utterance.

Some say, "I do not want to get 'in the flesh' when I receive the Holy Ghost." Well, you have to be in the flesh when you receive the Holy Ghost, for Peter said on the Day of Pentecost, "But this is that which was spoken by the prophet Joel; And it shall come to pass in the last days, saith God, I will pour out of my Spirit upon all flesh: and your sons and daughters shall prophesy, and your young men shall see visions, and your old men shall dream dreams." The Holy Spirit is poured out on men and women in the flesh, worshipping God in the Spirit. Praise God!

At this point, Brother Hagin gave an utterance in tongues. The following is the interpretation:

"Let thine ears be open, saith the Lord, thy mind, heart, and spirit receptive unto my Word, for the entrance of my Word will give you Light. And thou shall walk in the Light of the Word, so the desire, the hunger, and the thirst of thy spirit shall surely be satisfied. And ye shall receive the fulness of the Spirit and thy life shall be enriched."

Another utterance . . .

"Let no one say, 'I do not know, I cannot understand.' For surely my Word, saith the Lord, has been given unto thee and thou art without excuse for thou must walk in the Light. For it is written, 'If we walk in the Light as He is in the Light, we have fellowship one with another, and the blood of His Son cleanses us from all sin.'

"So surely, ye can walk in the Light, even the Light of the fulness of the Spirit, and thou shall enjoy an enlargement in thy spiritual life and thou shall enjoy the fulness of that which belongeth unto thee and another will not have to tell thee. For thou shall know for thyself the reality of His indwelling power."

Another utterance and interpretation:

"For thou art without excuse O Man, for thou art without excuse O Woman who hast said, 'I cannot understand these things and I do not know.' Thou hast thought in thy heart that what I don't know about, I will be excused for. But thou shall not be excused, saith the Lord of Host, for my Word is not just given to one here and one there, but my Word is given unto all. And I expect all believers to respond unto the Light. By so doing, thy life shall be enriched. The life of thy family shall be enriched. The life of those around and about you shall be enriched. And thou shalt enjoy that which thou hast hungered and longed for. But a refusal to walk in the Light of my Word can only bring thyself under condemnation and can only cause thy life to be cursed and the life of thy family to be under a curse, and the life of those around and about thee, instead of being blessed, to be cursed. Thou canst be a blessing or thou canst bring a curse. Walk ye in the Light, so thou shall be joyous, and the joy and the glow of the experience of my power shall flow out unto others to bless them also."

CHAPTER III

THE BIBLE WAY TO RECEIVE
THE HOLY SPIRIT

"And, behold, I send the promise of my Father upon you; but tarry ye in the city of Jerusalem, until ye be endued with power from on high" (Luke 24:49).

I want to say at the very outset of this message that I certainly do believe in tarrying. I certainly do believe in waiting on God. The word tarry means wait, and the Bible teaches us to wait on the Lord. The Bible says that they that wait upon the Lord shall renew their strength. Just because we are filled with the Holy Spirit is no sign that we shouldn't wait upon God. In fact, that is when one ought to begin to wait upon God — after he is filled with the Holy Ghost. As you wait upon the Lord, the Spirit of God can teach you, illuminate you, and guide you into all truth.

I not only believe it, but I practice what I preach. It will not help you in the least to believe a thing unless you put it into practice. I endeavor to practice waiting on God. In my meetings, there have been times when I waited on God four, five, or six hours. None of us will ever get to the place that we will not need to wait on God.

When it comes to being filled with the Holy Ghost, when I see our people who are waiting, praying, weeping, and agonizing, it breaks my heart, because I know they actually don't need to do that. Someone may ask, "Didn't Jesus say to tarry in Jerusalem until ye are endued with power from on high?"

Yes, He said that. But remember that Jesus said that to the disciples, before the day of Pentecost. If that is the divine pattern, why not take all of it? He said, "Tarry in the city of Jerusalem." If that is the divine formula, you would have to exhort individuals to go to Jerusalem to receive.

The one hundred and twenty in the Upper Room were not just exactly waiting or tarrying for the Holy Spirit. They were waiting for the Day of Pentecost. After the Day of Pentecost, there is not another example in the book of Acts where people tarried for the Holy Ghost.

Eight years after Pentecost, Philip went down to Samaria (Acts 8). As a result of his preaching, the people were saved and baptized in water. Then Peter and John laid hands on these Samaritans, "And they received the Holy Ghost" (Verse 17). Without agonizing, without tarrying, without disappointment, without exception, they were all filled with the Holy Ghost.

Ten years after Pentecost in Acts 10, Peter went to Caesarea to the house of Cornelius. Peter began to speak to them. Remember that "faith cometh by hearing, and hearing by the word of God." "While Peter yet spake these words, the Holy Ghost fell on all them which heard the word" (Verse 44), for "they heard them speak with tongues, and magnify God" (Verse 46). Cornelius, and his house, without praying, without waiting, without exception were filled with the Holy Ghost.

The Word of God tells us that twenty years after Pentecost (Acts 19), Paul passed through Ephesus and found certain Christians who had not heard "whether there be any Holy Ghost." Paul laid hands on them, and the "Holy Ghost came upon them; and they spake with tongues and prophesied." And the number of men "were about twelve." I don't know how many women and children were there. I want you to notice this: without waiting, without praying, without singing, every one of them was filled with the Holy Ghost.

Paul, the great apostle, received the Holy Ghost when Ananias laid hands on him (Acts 9:17). Though it does not say in that chapter that he spake with tongues, we know that he did, because Paul said later in I Corinthians 14:18, "I thank my God, I speak with tongues more than ye all."

In every instance in the Scripture when there was a group of people who wanted to receive the Holy Spirit, every single person was filled, and not one went away disappointed. If we taught our people in this day the same thing, then they would receive right away. God does not have any trial and error method. God does not have any method of coming, seeking and not finding, then going away empty.

Our people are so responsive, bless their dear hearts, that they believe what we tell them. It should be that way, but we should be careful that we are thoroughly Scriptural. I weigh heavily and with all earnestness what I say. When it comes to receiving the Holy Ghost, many have been so indefinite in instructing people.

Some time ago in another city I was staying in a parsonage while holding a meeting. It was an old house that had only recently been wired for electricity. My room didn't have a wall switch, only a string in the middle of the room. The living room did have a switch, and one night the pastor, after we had had a midnight snack, accidentally flipped the switch as he retired, which of course left me standing there in the dark as I was entering my room. I knew there was a string out there somewhere, and if I could just find it and pull it, I would have light. I went feeling for the string. About that time I hit my shins on the vanity bench. Then I came from another angle and ran into the door on the opposite side of the room. Next, I squared off against the door and ran into the bed post. I held on to the post, because I knew that it wasn't over three feet away from the light. Around and around I went, feeling for that string. Finally at long last, I struck the string with the side of my hand. I pulled the cord and there was light.

That's exactly what we have done. In trying to get people healed or filled, we tell them that there is a string out there somewhere, and when they feel it, to pull it, and that is it. That is the truth. Thank God some of them have found it, in spite of us, not because of us. It is a thousand wonders that we have gotten as many filled as we have.

A Baptist minister here in the state of Texas wanted to receive the Holy Spirit. Some told him to say, "Glory, glory."

Others said, "Say it faster." He got disgusted and quit because he couldn't find anything like that in the Word of God. When he saw what we preached was in the Word of God, he was filled with the Holy Ghost, speaking in other tongues. He brought a minister friend, and he was filled with the Holy Ghost. A Methodist minister received next. The revival was on! This is the Acts of the Apostles style. He went back to his own church, preached a two-week revival, and his own people received the Holy Ghost.

Jesus said, "If any man thirst, let him come unto me and drink." Just because you have been filled is no sign that you are not supposed to get thirsty any more. In the natural I am hungry and thirsty every day, and it is so in the spiritual realm. I feed on what I preach to you. What would you think of a cook that wouldn't eat her own cooking? "Man shall not live by bread alone, but by every word that proceedeth out of the mouth of God." The Word of God won't slack your thirst, but the Holy Ghost will. "Out of his belly shall flow rivers of living water."

Jesus did not say, "Let him come and shout." He didn't even say, "Let him come and pray" or "sweat, praise, prostrate," and go

26

away empty. He said, "Let him come and drink." We can drink every day and stay filled.

Paul said in I Corinthians 14:15, "I will pray with the spirit . . . I will sing with the spirit." Every Spirit-filled believer should be doing that every day in his private prayer life. Unless we are doing that, we are not keeping filled with the Spirit. If everyone did that, when we come to church the atmosphere would be charged.

How long does it take you to drink? How long do you have to pray before you can drink? How long do you have to sing before you can drink? If you can drink water, you can drink in the Spirit right now. Right now! Right now!

But some of us poor preachers testify and preach for 45 minutes about the Holy Ghost being here. Then after we get people to the altar, we say, "He isn't here. Lord, send him. Oh Lord, send the Power just now."

You say, "Brother Hagin, no use singing that anymore?"

You are right. No use singing that anymore. The Holy Ghost is here! The Holy Ghost isn't a reward. It is a gift.

One preacher said, "What you are preaching is Scriptural, but it is hard on some of us old fellows. I've been going one way so long, it's hard for me to change. I know I am wrong. I preached it as a reward. If it is a gift, then it is not a reward, and it is received by faith."

Someone asked, "Don't you think a fellow ought to straighten up his life before he gets filled with the Holy Ghost?" Bless God, if he's saved — born again — he's straight.

One fellow said, "I had to take a pig back I'd stolen before I could get the Holy Ghost."

I said, "I had to do that to get saved." We have so many foolish ideas. It's the truth. You can't buy the Holy Ghost with good works, and you can't pay cash for it. It is a gift. Besides that, doesn't the Bible say that the blood of Jesus Christ cleanses us from all sin? If a man is cleansed from all sin and is walking in the light, he is ready to be filled with the Holy Ghost, right now!

We have many silly notions about some things. One sister was praying for the Holy Ghost back in 1939. She was at one end of the altar, and the Lord baptized her. She spoke in other tongues. Later that evening as she had her hands upraised and was praising God in English, a man ran over to her and said, "Sister, pull your wedding ring off, and the Lord will fill you with the Holy Ghost." (That's what some people mean by straightening up.)

I answered him, "Brother, you're too late. He's already filled her, wedding band and all." Praise God! And He had!

Some say, "Brother Hagin, you make it just too easy." I always tell them that it wasn't I that did it. Thank God that it was God that did that.

Others say, "Yes, but I just don't believe in railroading them through." Well, do you believe in "railroading" people through to salvation? Certainly you do. If they don't get saved today, tomorrow may be too late. "Today is the day of salvation."

What do you mean by "railroading" them through? Well, getting them filled just as quickly as you can. Do you believe in railroading people through to healing? Don't you want to get healed as soon as you can, especially if you are in pain? Salvation is a gift; healing is a gift; the Holy Ghost is a gift. If they are all gifts and received by faith, then why tell a fellow that he has to wait?

One preacher remarked, "There's a lot of these 'new-fangled' methods. A lot of new short cuts. I believe in the old-fashioned way." Why friend, you can't get anymore old-fashioned than the Acts way, or the old time Bible way!

One minister said, "I waited for three years to get the Holy Ghost. I know that it means more to me than it would to have received quickly."

"Well," I answered, "poor old Paul. I wish that you could have gotten to him. I feel so sorry for poor old Paul. You said that the Holy Ghost doesn't mean anything to those that receive it quickly. Paul received it quickly. Ananias laid hands on him and he immediately received. But it didn't mean anything to him. All he ever did was write most of the New Testament. All he did was preach for thirty eight years where no one else had preached. He did more in thirty eight years than most denominations have done in five hundred years. If you could have gotten to Paul, he could have waited to be filled, and then maybe pastored a church that runs twenty-eight in Sunday school like yours." (I said that in love.)

But does it last? Whether you received it quickly or prayed a long time, it will last if you stay filled. Many of you were filled with the Holy Ghost five years ago. Well, if it lasts five years, it ought to be good for fifty years!

But someone remarked, "I remember those glorious times of

28

waiting on the Lord to be filled." Have you given up those times of waiting? I have an up-to-date experience. I remember the precious time I had waiting on the Lord last night. Glory!

Another said, "There have been more people filled with the Holy Ghost past midnight." The Bible doesn't say anything about past midnight. If they get filled past midnight, it's because they didn't believe before midnight. It is a gift! Friends, now is the time to receive. Come now, and receive the Water of the Spirit freely.

KENNETH HAGIN EVANGELISTIC ASSOCIATION
P.O. BOX 50126 • TULSA, OKLAHOMA 74150

Dear Friend,

I trust this book has been a blessing to you. We have endeavored to obey God and present the message He has given us in the printed word.

We are listing several books from our *Faith Library* which are of the same size and type as the one you have just read. God's message in them will enable the believer to fill to the utmost his place in the Body of Christ.

Redeemed From Poverty, Sickness and Death
What Faith Is
Seven Vital Steps to Receiving the Holy Spirit
Right and Wrong Thinking
Prayer Secrets
Authority of the Believer
How to Turn Your Faith Loose
Key to Scriptural Healing
The Ministry of a Prophet
The Origin and Operation of Demons
Demons and How to Deal With Them
Ministering to the Oppressed
Praying to Get Results
The Present Day Ministry of Jesus Christ
The Gift of Prophecy
Healing Belongs to Us
The Real Faith
Interceding Christian
How You Can Know the Will of God
Man on Three Dimensions
The Human Spirit

If you would like a complete list of all the materials available (study courses, group study books, cassettes, reel tapes, etc.) please write our office and request the *Faith Library Brochure*.

May God's richest and best be yours!

Kenneth E. Hagin

FAITH LIBRARY
STUDY COURSES

BIBLE FAITH STUDY COURSE

by Kenneth Hagin

Three large in-depth Study Courses are a part of the Faith Library by Kenneth Hagin. Each course contains 24 lessons, complete messages in themselves, bound in sturdy enamel covers. Quantity discounts are available. Single copy price per course is $5.00.

Some sample lesson titles from the BIBLE FAITH STUDY COURSE are: What Faith Is, The God Kind of Faith, How To Write Your Own Ticket With God, How To Train The Human Spirit, Confession Brings Possession.

BIBLE PRAYER STUDY COURSE

by Kenneth Hagin

Recognizing the vital need of an effective result-getting prayer life, Brother Hagin has often made the statement that if he were pastoring again, a prayer school where Believers could learn how to pray would be of top priority. In BIBLE PRAYER STUDY COURSE the fundamentals of an effective prayer life are covered in lessons such as: Praying For Results, Seven Steps to Answered Prayer, Praying in Jesus' Name, The Prayer of Faith, The Prayer of Worship, Praying With Tongues, The Will Of God In Prayer.

THE HOLY SPIRIT AND HIS GIFTS

by Kenneth Hagin

God's Holy Spirit has swept around the world and made His presence known in Believer's lives today as never before. You will gain insight into His personality and Gifts as you study lessons such as: The Holy Spirit Within, The Holy Spirit, An Ever-Present Source Of Power, Seven Steps To Receiving The Holy Spirit, Is It Scriptural to Tarry For The Holy Ghost, Ten Reasons Why Every Believer Should Speak In Tongues.

(To order courses or request quantity discount information, please write our office.)

KENNETH HAGIN EVANGELISTIC ASSOCIATION

P.O. BOX 50126 • TULSA, OKLAHOMA 74150

FAITH LIBRARY

Pocketbook Editions

I Believe in Visions

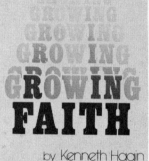

Exceedingly Growing Faith